3 3 3 3 3 3 3

For all those that believed

Just 3

Written and illustrated by Dee Fiffer

First Printing, 2024

Published by Mimiink

ISBN 978-I-7637603-0-I

Just three

Our life was perfect
Mum, Dad and me
Our life was perfect
when we were just three

We all liked to cook
Mum, Dad and me
and read all of our books
when we were just three

We played football in the park
Mum, Dad and me
then watched the stars when it turned dark
when we were just three

I loved the beach and building castles
with Mum, Dad and me
and we all helped carry the shopping parcels
when we were just three

At night we all went off to bed
Mum, Dad and me
they cuddled and kissed me on the head
when we were just three

We would go out to the park
and take our dog along
It all just seemed so perfect until
something went quite wrong

First they sat me down
Mum and Dad with me
they told me the shocking news
we wouldn't be just three

A baby was on the way
for Mum, Dad and me
but that would then make four
one extra, more than three

I panicked, stamped and cried
in front of Mum and Dad, yep that's me
I wanted to run and hide
what would happen to us three

Soon the big day had arrived
for Mum, Dad and me
and so I had a baby brother
the end of us just three

Now there are the four of us
Mum, Dad, me and my brother
I don't know why I made a fuss
I wouldn't want another

Sure, things are different round our house
for Mum, Dad and me
things are different round our house
but
Im glad there's four not three

4 4 4 4 4 4 4